The Slow Goodbye

The Slow Goodbye
copyright © 2024

All rights reserved. No part of this book may be reproduced or utilized in any form or by any means, electronic or mechanical, including photocopying, recording, or by any information storage and retrieval system, without written permission from the publisher.

Written by: Donesa Walker
Design by: Will Baten

DEDICATION

To all my dear friends and loved ones who have experienced this painful experience and loss.

Whose feet are those that are so large?

They look the size of a barge.

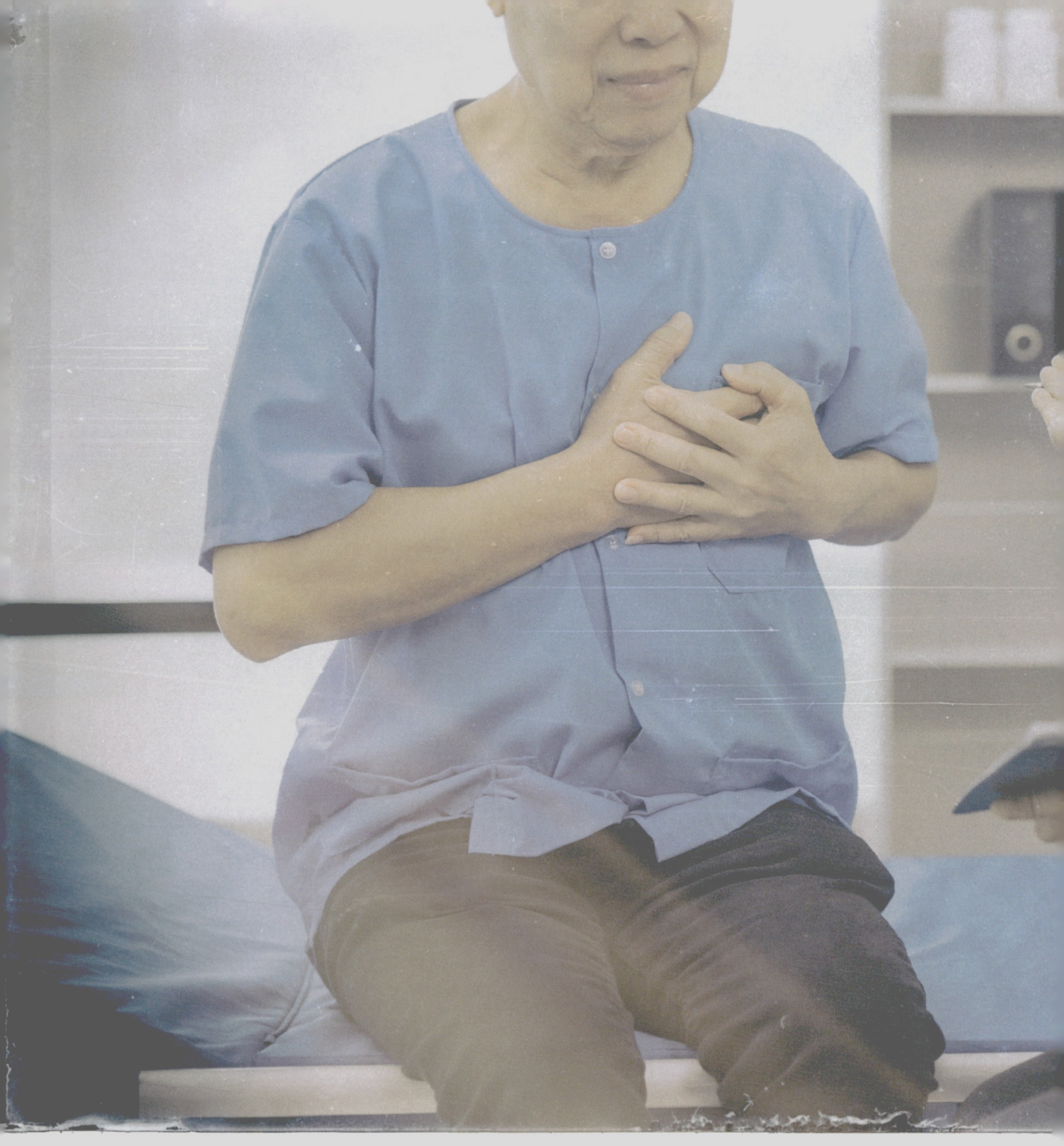

Who are these people staring at me?

Why won't they leave and let me be?

What is the time
and why am I here?

I look around in
constant fear.

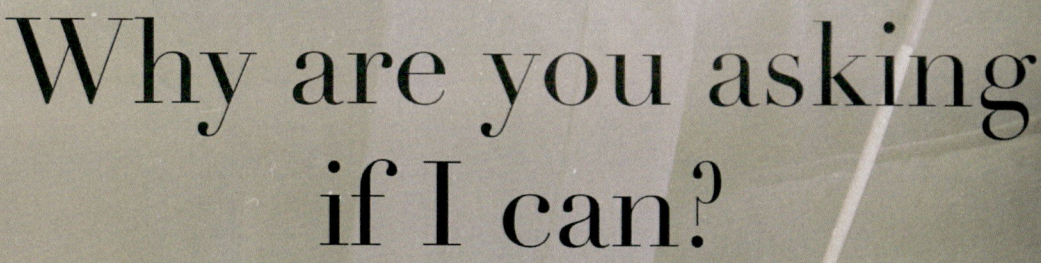

Why are you asking if I can?

Of course I will, just need a plan.

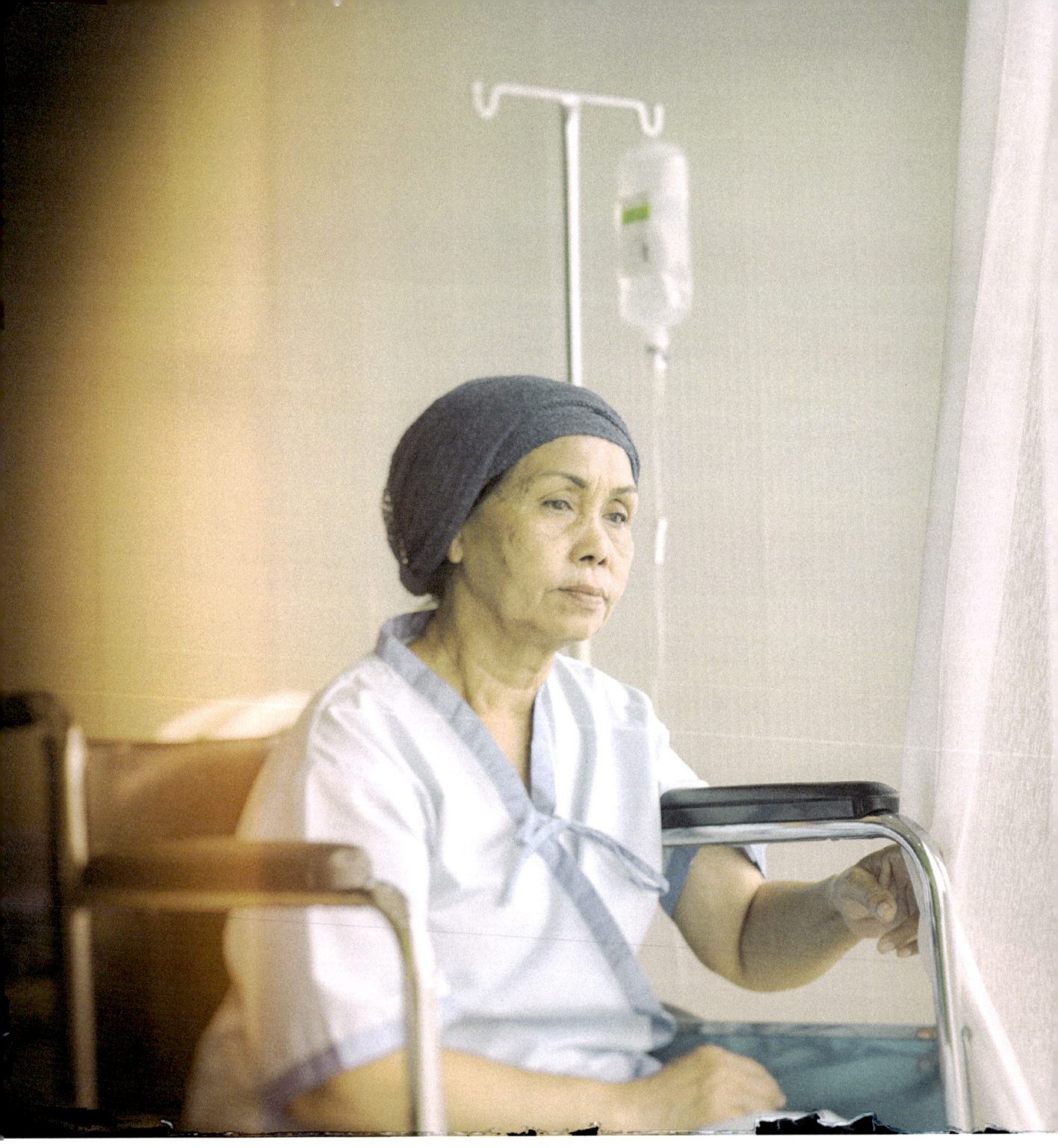

Who is the woman who has no hair?

Her baldness makes others stare.

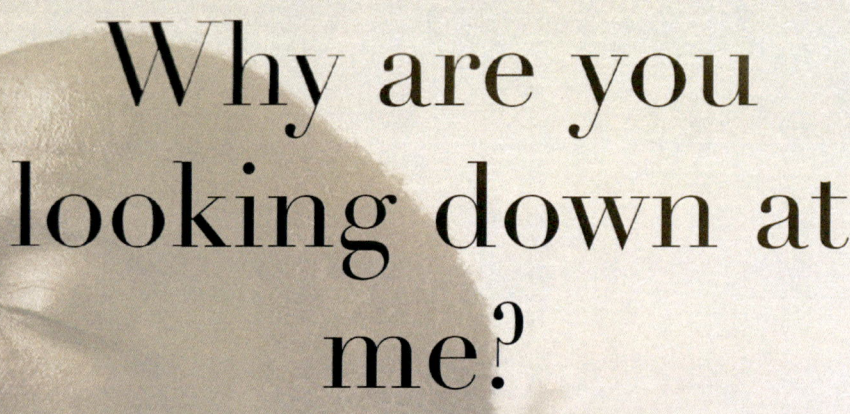

Why are you looking down at me?

I will get up just wait and see.

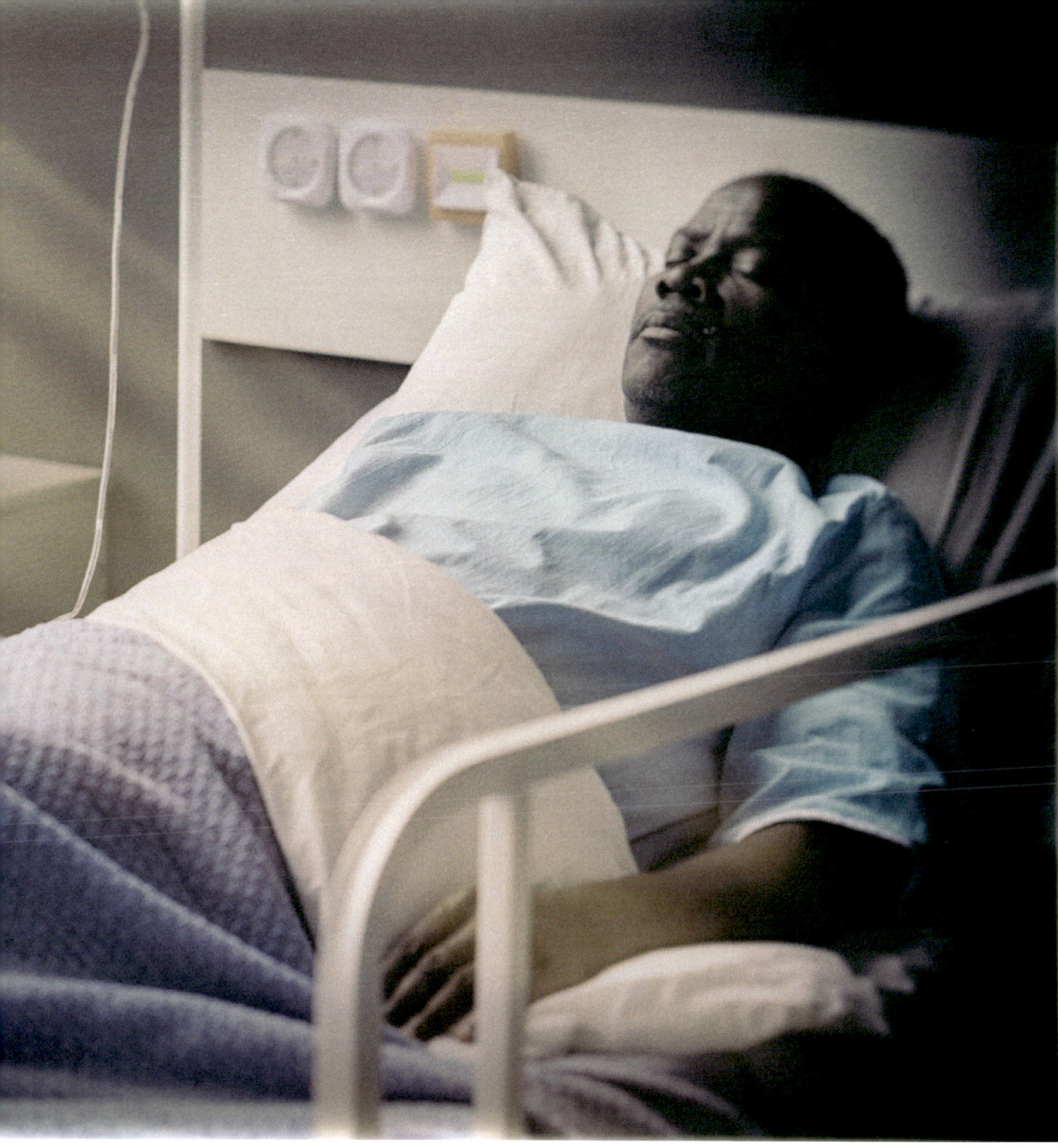

Why is that old man looking so rough?

This should not be. I've had enough.

The arms that used
to hold you high,
now cannot reach
into the sky.

The feet that used to take you places now cannot fit the shoes with laces.

The mind that used to hold so much now struggles to remember lunch.

The sharpest wit and finest heart now cannot seem to play the part.

The energy and drive of a strong back does not stop the sleeping lack.

The fittest heart and tightest abs did not stop cancer in its tracks.

My keenest skills and amazing rhythm couldn't stop the pain that's hidden.

The kindest smile and sweetest touch can not stop the anguish of an emotional crunch. Age is not my closest friend but I had no choice when he came in.

My time has come
way too fast and not
a moment will
I let pass.

Cherish the time through hurt and pain. Honor the love for eternal gain.

Life is fleeting and goes so quickly. Try not to be so nit picky.

Look on with love into that space, for time and memory, that will soon erase.

These moments here will pass too fast and only the memories will be here to last.

www.ingramcontent.com/pod-product-compliance
Lightning Source LLC
Chambersburg PA
CBRC091211010526
44119CB00021B/373